The Star and the Colours

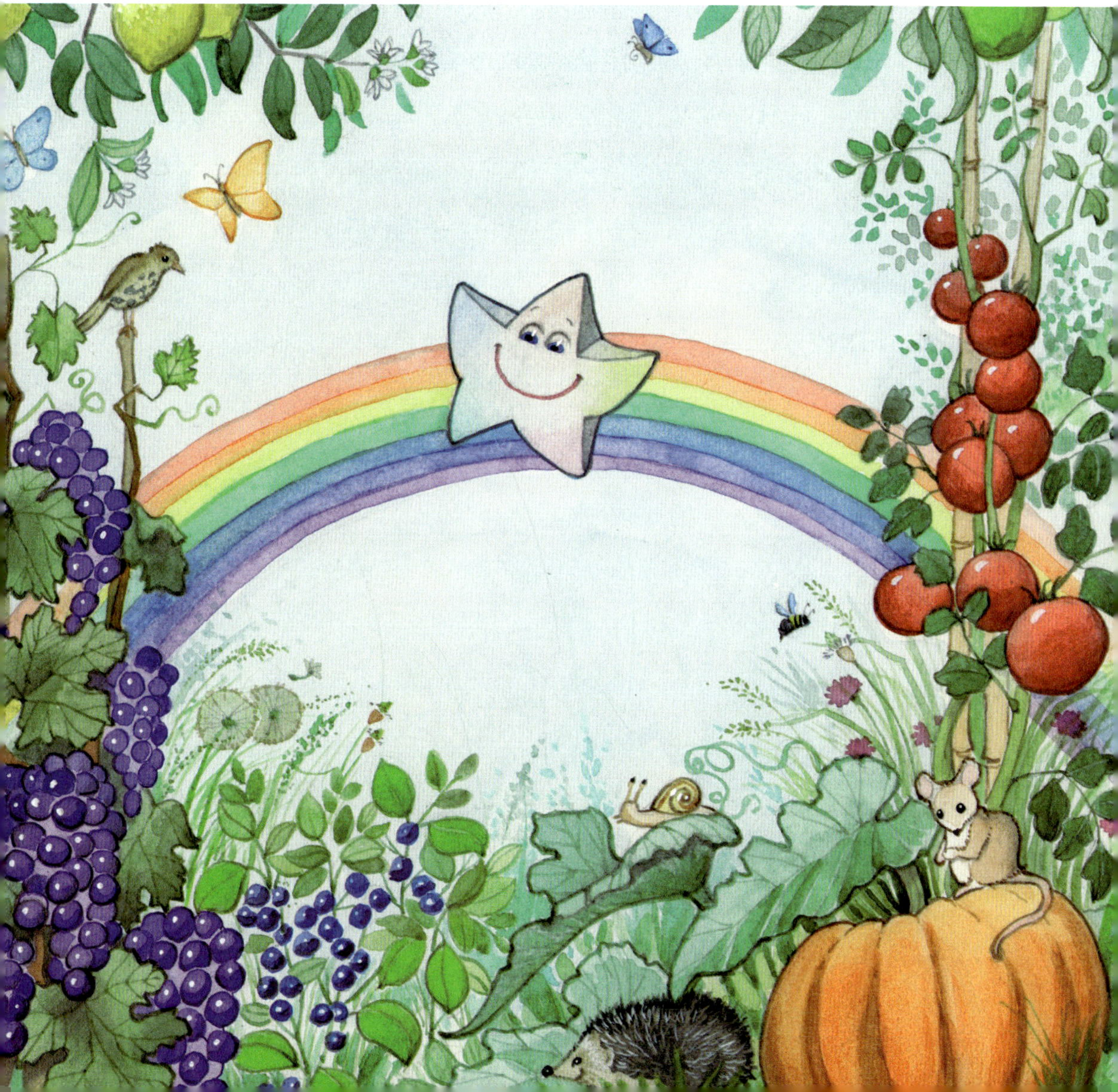

The night goes away.

The moon in the sky calls the stars.

'Come here!

It's time to go to bed!'

The stars go to bed.

But one star hides under a cloud.
She wants to see the sun.

The star waits.
'Where is the sun?' she says.
'I want to see the sun!'
Behind the mountains the sun comes out.
'Wow!' says the star, 'He's big!'
She looks around.
'What a lot of colours!'

'I see red tomatoes' says the star.
'I like red.
I want to be a red star!'
She sings a special song:

'Tiger, spider and bee!
This colour is for me!
One, two, three!'
But she isn't red.
'Oh,' says the star, 'this colour isn't for me.'
She looks around.

'I see orange pumpkins!' says the star.
'I like orange.
I want to be an orange star!'
She sings a special song:

'Tiger, spider and bee,
this colour is for me!
One, two, three.'
But she isn't orange!
'Oh,' says the star 'this colour isn't for me.'
She looks around.

'I see yellow lemons!' says the star.

'I like yellow.

I want to be a yellow star!'

She sings a special song:

'Tiger, spider and bee,

this colour is for me!

One, two, three.'

But she isn't yellow!

'Oh,' says the star 'this colour isn't for me.'

She looks around.

'I see green apples!' says the star.
'I like green.
I want to be a green star!'

She sings a super song!
'Coffee, toffee and tea,
this colour is for me!
One, two, three.'
But she isn't green!
'Oh,' says the star 'this colour isn't for me.'
She looks around.

'I see little blueberries!' says the star.
I like blue.
I want to be a blue star!'
She sings a super song!
'Coffee, toffee and tea,
this colour is for me!
One, two, three.'
But she isn't blue!
'Oh,' says the star 'this colour isn't for me.'
She looks around.

'I see purple and violet grapes!' says the star.

I like purple and violet.

I want to be a purple and violet star!'

She sings a super song!

'Coffee, toffee and tea,

this colour is for me!

One, two, three.'

But she isn't purple or violet!

'Oh,' says the star 'these colours aren't for me.'

She looks around.

'I see big clouds' says the star.
'Where is the sun?
I want to see the sun!'

18

'Oh no!' says the star,
'Pitter patter, pitter patter!
There are raindrops on my head!
I want a hat!'

19

The star is cold and tired.
She falls asleep.
PITTER PATTER, PITTER PATTER!
It rains on the mountains
and it rains on the star.
PITTER PATTER, PITTER PATTER!
It rains and then it stops.
The clouds go away.

The sun comes out.
He is big and hot.
The star opens her eyes and sees the sun.
'Wow!' she says.
And from her mouth a big rainbow comes out: red, orange, yellow, green, blue, purple and violet!
'Hurray!' says the star
'These colours are for me!'

Where is the sun?

1 Help the star to find the sun.

What a lot of colours!

2 Read and colour the star.

1 I ♥ red. I want to be a red ⭐

2 I ♥ orange. I want to be an orange ⭐

3 I ♥ yellow. I want to be a yellow ⭐

4 I ♥ green. I want to be a green ⭐

5 I ♥ blue. I want to be a blue ⭐

6 I ♥ purple and violet. I want to be a purple and violet ⭐

Fruit and vegetables

3 **Read and match.**

4 Read and find the odd one out.

grapes	rain	blueberries	apple
red	mountain	yellow	purple
one	cloud	two	three
head	mouth	sun	eyes

A special star

5 Make a special star

You need:

A star shape 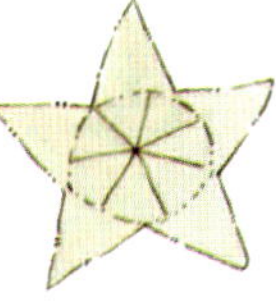   Scissors 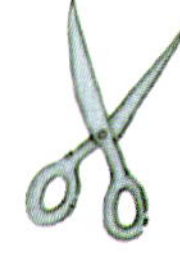

Felt-tip pens 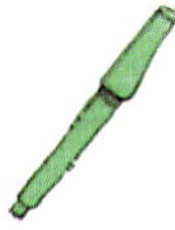   A pencil 

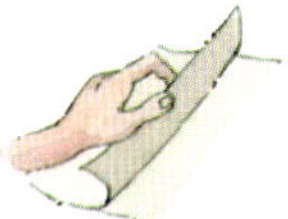

Turn the page and make a special star!

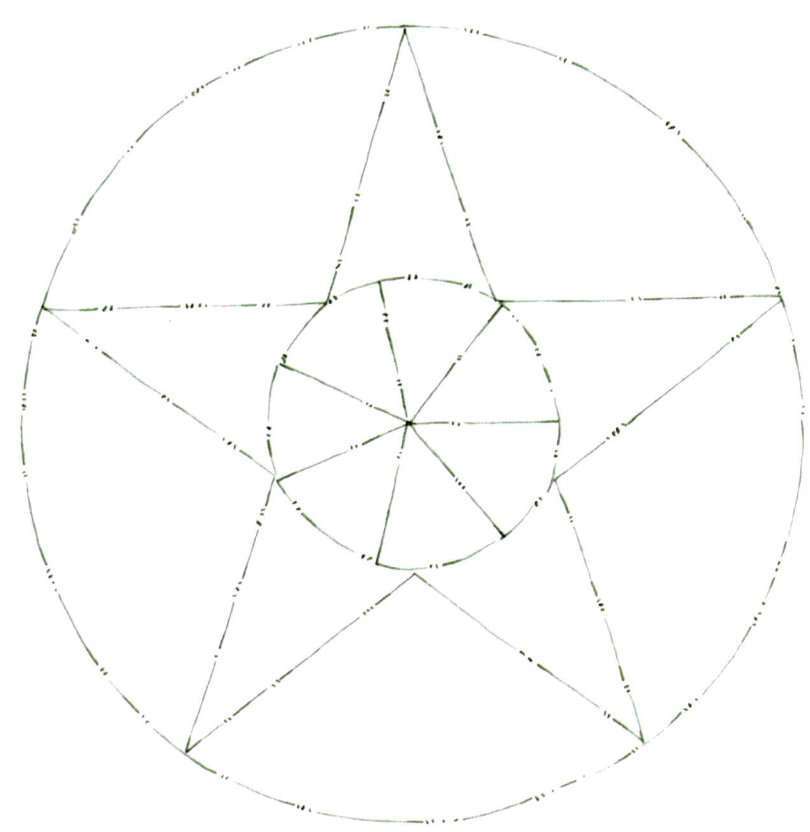

1 Cut out the star

2 Colour the circle red, yellow, green, blue, purple and violet

3 Put a pencil through the centre of the star

4 Spin and look!

Picture Dictionary

night 

sky 

star 

moon 

mountain 

sun 

cloud 

rain 

raindrops 

rainbow

lemon  

apple 

blueberries 

grapes 

tomato 

pumpkin 

toffee 

coffee 

tea 

tiger
spider
bee
hide
wait
STOP
WAIT
GO
come out
come here
go away
look around
see
sing
open
go to bed
fall asleep
tired
hat
head
eyes
mouth

big

little

hot

cold

in

on

under

behind

Key

Activity 1

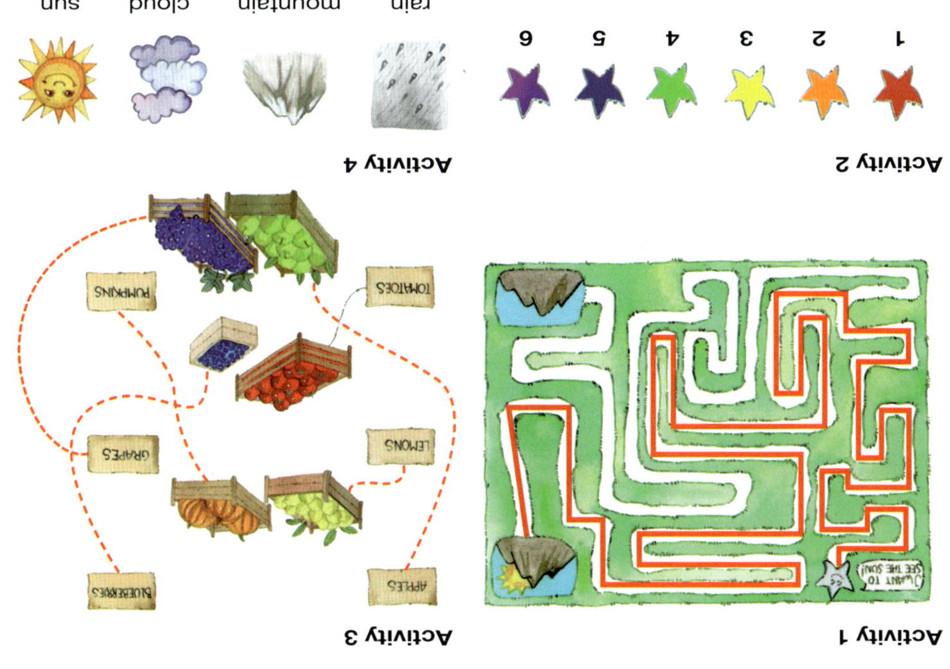

Activity 2

1 2 3 4 5 6

Activity 3

Activity 4

rain   mountain   cloud   sun

Editor: Robert Hill

Design and art direction: Nadia Maestri

Computer graphics: Carlo Cibrario-Sent, Simona Corniola

© 2012 Black Cat

First edition: January 2012

DEALINK, DEAFLIX are trademarks licensed by
De Agostini SpA

All rights reserved. No part of this book may be reproduced,
stored in a retrieval system, or transmitted,
in any form or by any means, electronic, mechanical,
photocopying, recording or otherwise, without the written
permission of the publisher.

We would be happy to receive your comments and
suggestions, and give you any other information concerning
our material.
info@blackcat-cideb.com
blackcat-cideb.com

The Publisher is certified by

CISQCERT

in compliance with the UNI EN ISO 9001:2008
standards for the activities of «Design and
production of educational materials»
(certificate no. 02.565)

Printed in Italy by Litoprint, Genoa